MW00805564

THE POWER OF THE HOLY SPIRIT'S NAMES

TONY EVANS

HARVEST HOUSE PUBLISHERS
EUGENE, OREGON

Unless otherwise indicated, all Scripture quotation are taken from the (NASB®) New American Standard Bible®, Copyright © 1960, 1971, 1977, 1995 by The Lockman Foundation. Used by permission. All rights reserved. www.lockman.org.

Cover design by Faceout Studios, Spencer Fuller

Cover Photo © Sentavio, Sandra_M / Shutterstock

Interior design by KUHN Design Group

For bulk, special sales, or ministry purchases, please call 1-800-547-8979. Email: Customerservice@hhpbooks.com

The Power of the Holy Spirit's Names Workbook
Copyright © 2022 by Tony Evans
Published by Harvest House Publishers
Eugene, Oregon 97408
www.harvesthousepublishers.com

ISBN 978-0-7369-7965-8 (pbk.)
ISBN 978-0-7369-7966-5 (eBook)

Printed in the United States of America

22 23 24 25 26 27 28 29 30 / BP / 10 9 8 7 6 5 4 3 2 1

CONTENTS

I want to thank my friends at Harvest House Publishers for their long-standing partnership in bringing my thoughts, study, and words to print. I particularly want to thank Bob Hawkins for his friendship over the years as well as for his pursuit of excellence in leading his company. I also want to publicly thank Kim Moore for her help in the editorial process.

Working with the team at RightNow Media is always a pleasure, and they bring great professionalism and talent to what they do as well as a love for our Lord. Thank you, Phil Warner, for leading your group so well, and many thanks to the entire team that filmed and edited this study. In addition, my appreciation goes to Heather Hair for her skills and insights in collaboration on this Bible study content and assistance with the video production.

MAKING THE MOST OF THIS WORKBOOK/PARTICIPANT'S GUIDE

This workbook and guide is a tool to help your group combine the video and subsequent Bible study into a dynamic growth experience. If you are the leader or facilitator of your group, take some time in advance to consider the questions in the Video Group Discussion and Group Bible Exploration sections of this guide, and then come up with personal examples to encourage discussion. Also make sure each individual has their own workbook, which will allow them to take notes during the group time as well as dig deeper on their own throughout the week.

Because every group session includes a video portion, think about the logistics. Before the session, ensure that everyone will be able to see the screen clearly and that the audio is set at a comfortable level. You don't want your group to miss anything.

Now let's preview the sections in each of the six sessions.

Video Teaching Notes

Several key points and quotes from the video are provided in this section, and room to write notes is also provided.

Video Group Discussion

Many of the discussion questions have to do with remembering what was just viewed, and this immediate follow-up is important; we can forget content unless we review it right away. Other questions in this section try to connect the video to emotions or experience. *How did you feel when Tony said that? Is that true in your life? Do you have the same issue?*

Group Bible Exploration

This is a Bible study, so each session is grounded in Scripture. And because different levels of faith may be found within your group, this time in the Bible is not only to grow, but to also help others find their faith.

In Closing

The goal for every Bible study is to apply what's learned. This section highlights the main point of the session and challenges participants to dive deeper.

On Your Own Between Sessions

This section includes additional study participants can do to keep the content they just learned fresh in their minds throughout the week and encourages them to put it into practice.

Recommended Reading

Your group time will be enhanced if everyone reads the recommended chapters in *The Power of the Holy Spirit's Names* book by Tony Evans before the next session. Tony's video teaching follows the book, but the book has considerably more information and illustrations. Everyone is encouraged to prepare ahead by reading the designated chapters.

THE HELPER

The following is an excerpt from *The Power of the Holy Spirit's Names* book, serving as an introduction to the Holy Spirit and then focusing on Him as the Helper.

The Holy Spirit is the most misunderstood, marginalized, misused, and under-appreciated member of the Trinity. On the one hand, He's ignored, and on the other hand, He's illegitimately sensationalized. Both extremes cancel or limit His work in and through God's people. That's why it's important for us to not only know the Holy Spirit more but as He really is.

The Spirit has a central role in the life of the believer and the empowerment of the church, with the distinctive task of making the reality and truth of God experienced in both. And because He possesses emotions, intellect, and will, He is to be related to on a personal level. He's to be *known*, not merely considered a force or power to be manipulated or used. Although He's nonmaterial, intangible, and invisible, He is nonetheless real and relational.

As with the other two members of the Trinity, one of the best means to understand, appreciate, and benefit from the person of the Holy Spirit is to explore the names and attribute descriptions He's given in Scripture. They explain how He lives those roles in us, through us, and for us.

My first goal in this book, then, is to identify, explain, and illustrate the Holy Spirit and His work through those descriptions and names. By the way, while some of the Holy Spirit's names and descriptions are not always capitalized as proper nouns as I write — just as they aren't in Scripture or at least in some Bible translations or paraphrases — they are nevertheless as significant to our study as if they were.

A second goal is to show believers how to relate to the person of the Holy Spirit in a more personal and intimate way. And a third goal is to help us learn how to take full advantage of all the Spirit offers for our physical lives, our emotional lives, and most importantly, our spiritual lives. When we grasp how to do this, His availability can be maximized for our personal and collective growth and impact.

When we come to know the Spirit—again, not only more but as He really is—we can more intimately tap into the unique ways God reveals Himself to us. That's why we all need to understand that to the degree we take the person and work of the Holy Spirit seriously is the degree to which we will experience more of God…

Some English translations of Scripture don't use the word *Helper*. They use words like *Advocate* or *Comforter*. This is because the Greek term *parakletos* encompasses the Spirit's meeting all these "helping" needs, depending on the situation. God chose for the New Testament's inspired writers to define the Holy Spirit according to this particular name because it can fit a variety of circumstances and needs. It's a flexible term, so fluid that it more accurately reflects the Holy Spirit's ability to help us in times of need.

If you're depressed, the Holy Spirit can help you with encouragement. If you're discouraged, He can help you with new strength. If you're afraid, He can help you by calming your fears. If you're struggling, He can even ease the struggle. And if you're alone, the Holy Spirit can be your friend. He can flex to whatever situation you're in and whatever you need.

The Power of the Holy Spirit's Names, pages 9-10, 19-20

Video Teaching Notes

As you watch the video, use the space below to take notes. Some key points and quotes are provided as reminders.

Main Idea

- In His identity as the *paraklete*, the Holy Spirit serves believers as our divine Helper. He knows what we need, when we need it, and how to meet that need. The Holy Spirit carries on Jesus' will on earth now that He is ascended to the Father. He helps us live out our calling as kingdom followers of Christ.

- In the context of the upper room, just before His arrest and crucifixion, Jesus comforts His disciples. He tells them in John 14:1, "Do not let your heart be troubled." Jesus knew He would be going away, but He also knew He was about to send a Helper, the Holy Spirit (John 14:16-17).

- The Holy Spirit softened the blow and shock of Jesus' leaving the disciples' presence.

He came to immediately provide what they needed right then and to all of us who would live after them.

> » The Holy Spirit would teach "all things" (John 14:26).

> » The Holy Spirit would "testify" about Jesus (John 15:26).

> » The Holy Spirit would guide into "all truth" (John 16:13).

- Personal Notes:

Application

Your relationship with the Holy Spirit is a two-way connection, you with Him and He with you. Move toward the Spirit, remain in touch with Him, and watch what He will do. Pray consistently, study Scripture regularly, and turn to God in times of need.

Quotables

- The word *help* is used as a summary term for all the variables the Holy Spirit can provide.

- This is the age of the Holy Spirit. As Jesus came to earth and was the visible manifestation of God, the Holy Spirit has now come to earth, the manifestation of Christ in history.

- With the Holy Spirit, we all have equal access to God and equal access to Jesus Christ.

Video Group Discussion

1. In the video, Tony touched on some seasons or experiences in life when we may need help. He mentioned needing a mechanic if your car is broken or an accountant if your finances are out of whack. What are some other activities where you may need help? How do you feel about asking for help?

2. In the opening of the video, Tony said, "God has supplied someone whose job it is to come alongside you in the various areas of your life." Why is it important to realize the role of the Spirit as a helper?

3. Look at a passage referenced in the video, John 14:16-17, and reflect on this Scripture in light of the following points of emphasis:

   • *Forever.* Read also Matthew 6:13: "Do not lead us into temptation, but deliver us from evil. [For Yours is the kingdom and the power and the glory forever. Amen."]

     How does this passage in John align with the provision of the Spirit as Helper from a time standpoint?

     Why is it important to know that the Spirit's help is not transient, offered for only a short time, but available forever?

   • *Freedom.* Read also John 8:32 — "You will know the truth, and the truth will make you free."

     Can you think of a time when you experienced the freeing power of the truth and share it? What did that experience do to your desire to know truth and overcome the devil's deception?

   • *Fruit.* Read also John 15:4 — "Abide in Me, and I in you. As the branch cannot bear fruit of itself unless it abides in the vine, so neither can you unless you abide in Me."

The word *abide* reflects intimacy and positioning. Describe what it means to you to abide in Jesus. Then describe what it means to you to abide in the Spirit.

How does knowing that God produces spiritual fruit as you abide in Him inspire and encourage you to abide?

4. In the video, Tony said the term *paraclete* "can mean counselor. It can mean comforter. It can mean advocate. It can mean assistant. The word can flow based on the situation that's needed." How does gaining clarity on the Holy Spirit's various roles as Helper open your mind to His value in your life?

List three ways you can seek to make better use of the Holy Spirit's help.

1.

2.

3.

Once a greater reliance on the Holy Spirit's help is established and tapped into, what can result?

5. Read the verses on page 12 and describe how each one relates to the role of the Holy Spirit as Helper in our lives.

1 Corinthians 12:4,11 — "Now there are varieties of gifts, but the same Spirit…But one and the same Spirit works all these things, distributing to each one individually just as He wills."

Acts 1:8 — "You will receive power when the Holy Spirit has come upon you; and you shall be My witnesses both in Jerusalem, and in all Judea and Samaria, and even to the remotest part of the earth."

1 Corinthians 2:13 — "We also speak, not in words taught by human wisdom, but in those taught by the Spirit, combining spiritual thoughts with spiritual words."

Knowing that the Holy Spirit has come to offer us help in so many ways ought to increase our interest in and focus on Him. He is a gift from God sent from above so that we will have all we need to fully live out the victorious kingdom life.

Group Bible Exploration

1. Read the following verses and explore what they tell you about the Holy Spirit's ability to help in a person's life. Then share a practical example of what that might look like in a contemporary setting. Feel free to make it a personal testimony.

    Romans 15:13 — "Now may the God of hope fill you with all joy and peace in believing, so that you will abound in hope by the power of the Holy Spirit."

    Help Given:

Practical Example:

Acts 2:4 — "They were all filled with the Holy Spirit and began to speak with other tongues, as the Spirit was giving them utterance."

Help Given:

Practical Example (you may want to expand your thinking outside of speaking other languages):

Acts 4:31 — "When they had prayed, the place where they had gathered together was shaken, and they were all filled with the Holy Spirit and began to speak the word of God with boldness."

Help Given:

Practical Example:

2. The Trinity is made up of three co-equal persons: the Father, the Son, and the Holy Spirit. Each one has a distinct role. As we saw in our introduction to the Holy Spirit, one of His roles is to provide help when we need it most.

Four key verses in Scripture enable us to gain a greater understanding of this role. Read each verse on page 14, and then reflect on what it means to you personally. Write down your thoughts and summary of each verse in the space provided.

- John 14:16 — "I will ask the Father, and He will give you another Helper, that He may be with you forever."

- John 14:26 — "The Helper, the Holy Spirit, whom the Father will send in My name, He will teach you all things, and bring to your remembrance all that I said to you."

- John 15:26 — "When the Helper comes, whom I will send to you from the Father, that is the Spirit of truth who proceeds from the Father, He will testify about Me."

- John 16:7 — "I tell you the truth, it is to your advantage that I go away; for if I do not go away, the Helper will not come to you; but if I go, I will send Him to you."

As a Christian, you have never been alone. From the moment you trusted in Jesus Christ for salvation from your sins, you received the companionship of the Holy Spirit externally and internally. The reason the Holy Spirit remains present in both places is that, depending on the situation, you can need help in both areas of your life. Whether you're facing something in your external circumstances or struggling with internal thoughts or emotions, the Holy Spirit has positioned Himself to be available to you when and where you need Him the most. He is your helper and ready to help—all you need to do is ask.

3. Read Matthew 7:7 — "Ask, and it will be given to you; seek, and you will find; knock, and it will be opened to you."

In what ways do you take comfort in knowing the help of the Holy Spirit is as close to you as asking for it?

Have you ever considered this verse in connection with the Holy Spirit? Why or why not?

Why do you think God puts an emphasis on our role in asking for help when we need it rather than simply supplying the help He knows we need?

In Closing

As you end the study today, share prayer requests related to seeking the Holy Spirit's help in your life and your desire to cultivate your relationship with Him. Be specific about the areas you feel you most need to grow in and develop. Ask the Holy Spirit to open your hearts throughout this study so you can come to know Him like never before. Also ask Him to guard and protect your priorities, time, and passions to enable each of you to finish this study in its entirety.

Before session 2, complete the "On Your Own Between Sessions" section below.

On Your Own Between Sessions

1. In the book, Tony goes into greater detail on the Holy Spirit's role in our lives as a valued helper, distinguishing Him from an impersonal Being to who He truly is. He wrote,

The Holy Spirit, as the third person of the Trinity, is not an "it." He's not just a "power" to turn on and use, although we'll later see that power is one of His attributes. He's a person present both alongside each of us and within us. And as a person, He desires for you to relate to Him as much as anyone else would want you to relate to them.

He also possesses intellect, emotion, and volition. He's not a robot where you get to push buttons and He obeys. He is not AI. The Holy Spirit exists as a relational Being formed of an immaterial essence in order to abide both with you and in you throughout your life.

One of the reasons we don't witness His help as much as we could is that we have relegated Him to robotic status. We've viewed Him as something to use, not Someone to know. If anyone in your life just wants to use you and clearly doesn't care about you, you know how your heart turns away from helping them. But that's often how we relate to the Holy Spirit.

My point here is that too often believers just want to use Him at will. And unless you and I truly understand and explore ways to relate to the Spirit and engage with Him, we will never fully experience the benefits He makes available to us.

The Power of the Holy Spirit's Names, pages 22-23

Read Isaiah 11:2 and then Zechariah 4:6:

- The Spirit of the LORD will rest on Him,
  The spirit of wisdom and understanding,
  The spirit of counsel and strength,
  The spirit of knowledge and the fear of the LORD.

- Then he said to me, "This is the word of the LORD to Zerubbabel saying, 'Not by might nor by power, but by My Spirit,' says the LORD of hosts."

The Holy Spirit works in myriad ways to provide help when we need it most. It's the Spirit's power that enables us to live out the will of God in our lives. What are some ways you've witnessed the Spirit help you accomplish things too big for you to accomplish on your own?

What are some things in your life that might hinder you from looking to the Holy Spirit for help? They could be distractions or emotions.

What can you do to lessen these distractions or better inform these emotions? Will you try? Why or why not?

2. Isaiah 11:2 (see above in question 1) lists a number of descriptive terms for the Holy Spirit. Describe each one in your own words.

Draw from those descriptions to form your own definition of the Holy Spirit's role as Helper.

3. The Holy Spirit longs to help you. He loves you. He seeks an abiding relationship with you. What are some things you can do to better cultivate your relationship with the Holy Spirit?

The Holy Spirit desires a personal relationship with you. He doesn't want to be considered a robot who performs at your command. How does knowing that the Spirit desires your focus and heart to be set on Him make you feel?

Ask the Spirit to enlighten your eyes in order to see Him more clearly. Seek to come to know Him more than you do now or have known Him in the past. Spend regular time recalling the ways the Spirit has helped you in the past, and then thank Him for that help.

4. Life Exercise: Getting Intimate with the Holy Spirit

Identify a time when you can spend concentrated and focused energy on your relationship with and communication with the Holy Spirit.

Consider several ways to nurture your relationship with the Holy Spirit during this season of focus on Him. That might mean writing freely about what you're thinking concerning the Spirit or what you sense you're hearing from Him in a notebook. Or it could mean reading the Word of God and meditating on the various manifestations of the Holy Spirit recorded in it.

Evaluate how your relationship deepens as you spend more focused time reflecting on the power and presence of the Holy Spirit.

Repeat in the weeks to come. Incorporate the various aspects we're studying about the power of the Holy Spirit's names into your daily intimate time with God.

Recommended Reading

In preparation for session 2, please read chapters 2–5 of *The Power of the Holy Spirit's Names* book.

THE LORD

The following is an excerpt from *The Power of the Holy Spirit's Names* book, focusing on the Holy Spirit as the Lord.

If you've ever been to a carnival or amusement park, you may have come across the traditional house of mirrors, where the mirrors distort what they reflect. They're shaped in such a way that they make you look extremely tall, wide, small, or lopsided. Your physical body takes on a whole new shape and look based on the mirror reflecting it.

Similarly, a distorted soul leads to a distorted self-image that produces distorted words and actions that damage lives. Of course, this distortion is expressed at different degrees and levels of intensity, but it's expressed by all of us no matter how hard we try to mask it.

All of that is tough news to swallow, but God has good news. He's provided all we need to address the sin operating within our flesh. As you might imagine since we're focusing on the Holy Spirit in this book, the solution to our sin problem lies with the Holy Spirit.

We read about this in 2 Corinthians 3:17-18:

> Now the Lord is the Spirit, and where the Spirit of the Lord is, there is liberty. But we all, with unveiled face, beholding as in a mirror the glory of the Lord, are being transformed into the same image from glory to glory, just as from the Lord, the Spirit.

Notice the words *but we all* in the passage. These three words are very important, because they indicate no exceptions exist. That said, you are not an exception. God's solution is perfect for anyone who will use it. No matter what you may have thought, said, or done, God can turn your life around when you tap into the power of the Holy

Spirit. The Spirit has the strength to address the damage done to your soul from your childhood, exacerbated by your circumstances and then irritated by your own actions.

And so we find the Spirit's strength as we uncover another of His names—the Lord. Now, you may think this is an odd name to call the Holy Spirit since Jesus is frequently known as Lord. But that's why it's important to truly study the Holy Spirit. We have far too frequently relegated Him to one role—that of emotionalism, all the while ignoring or downplaying His myriad other roles.

Jesus Christ is no longer physically on earth; He is physically in heaven. But if you're a believer, He is spiritually in you. Yet we often forget that in this process of Jesus taking up residence in each of us spiritually, He does so through the agency of the Holy Spirit.

The Lord is the Spirit. And as we saw in the passage earlier, "where the Spirit of the Lord is, there is liberty." The term *liberty* indicates release from anything or anyone holding you illegitimately hostage—whether a relationship, a habit, an attitude, a belief, or a situation. Whatever it is, you need to realize that you have the Spirit, who is Jesus the Lord, inside of you to release you. A release mechanism is operating inside you because where the Spirit of the Lord is, there is freedom to be found.

The Spirit of the Lord releases you from bondage through one specific strategy: He transforms you from the inside out.

The Power of the Holy Spirit's Names, pages 79-81

Video Teaching Notes

As you watch the video, use the space below to take notes. Some key points and quotes are provided as reminders.

Main Idea

- Because the Spirit is fully God—our Lord—those indwelt by the Spirit have direct access to God. We can be transformed from our old way of life and freed to become what God intended when we tap into the power of the Spirit. Only through intimate authenticity and vulnerability with the Spirit will we grow more like Jesus.

- Access to God leads to freedom from behaviors, situations, and people that keep us apart from Him.

- Freedom that comes from the Spirit inside us leads to transformation; the Lord is working in us effecting change and greater holiness. If we're not changing, we're not growing spiritually. Transformation takes place when we actively participate, obeying

God's Word and not just hearing it, as our true selves. No hiding, no pretending (James 1:19-25).

• Personal Notes:

Application

It's time to get real with God, to be honest with Him about your struggles, temptations, and questions. Spend time in His Word. Notice what He says to do that you might not be doing or what He says not to do that you need to stop doing. Ask the Spirit to give you strength, wisdom, and maturity as you seek to walk in His ways.

Quotables

• Your spirit, infused by the Holy Spirit and based on the Word of God, infuses your soul.

• What the Holy Spirit wants to do is…bring the experience of God into your reality.

• When [the Holy Spirit] kicks in, He begins to make the changes needed so that we begin to experience God in reality and not merely in theory.

Video Group Discussion

1. Tony begins this session talking about where he's filming. He's standing in a location called the "Cathedral of Junk" located in Austin, Texas. This cathedral exists because one man decided to transform trash into a treasure. He started many years ago with a small exhibit here or there in the backyard, but over time he's created such a beautiful place that hundreds of thousands of people flock there just to tour it. Looking at your life, on a scale of 1 to 10, with 10 being the most, how much of the trash, mess, and yuck of your past has God turned into a treasure?

   1 -- 10

2. In what ways might we hinder the process of the Holy Spirit's work of life transformation?

3. What are some things that keep us from releasing past shame, guilt, or blame and allowing God to make a miracle out of our mess? (Examples might be apathy, doubt, or embarrassment.)

4. In what ways can we help the process of transforming the trials of our lives into testimonies?

5. In the video, Tony gives the illustration of how different men and women can be when it comes to mirrors. Men will often glance in a mirror while women may stare. Or women might have more than one mirror placed here or there to use throughout the day. When God says we are to look at His Word deeply and intently, He warns us against glancing at it like a man glances in a mirror (James 1:23-24).

Can a glance at God's Word bring about true lasting life transformation? Why or why not?

On another scale from 1 to 10, where would you rate your attention to God's Word (1 being "I glance" and 10 being "I dive deep")?

1 --10

Describe any parallels or contrasts between your answers on the two scales (question #1 and question #5).

6. Identify how a greater abiding in the Word of God as well as a closer intimacy with the Holy Spirit could lead to spiritual growth in your life. In what areas would you like to see the Holy Spirit more involved when it comes to your daily activities, difficulties, sins, or temptations?

Group Bible Exploration

1. Freedom affords each of us the opportunity to live out our destiny and purpose as God created us to do. But this freedom comes from God Himself, through the Spirit. This principle is laid out for us in 2 Corinthians 3:17, which we read in our opening time together. Turn back to page 19 to review this passage, then answer the following questions.

Why do we often mistakenly connect liberty (freedom) with license?

How can we embrace living a life of freedom while continuing to honor God with our choices?

When God liberates us through freedom, what does He intend to liberate us from?

2. Compare and combine principles in 2 Corinthians 3:18 with 1 Thessalonians 5:23:

2 Corinthians 3:18 — "We all, with unveiled face, beholding as in a mirror the glory of the Lord, are being transformed into the same image from glory to glory, just as from the Lord, the Spirit."

1 Thessalonians 5:23 — "Now may the God of peace Himself sanctify you entirely; and may your spirit and soul and body be preserved complete, without blame at the coming of our Lord Jesus Christ."

Based on these two verses, what are the transformational goals God is seeking to do in each of us?

In your own words, what does it mean to be "preserved complete"?

How might the principles in these two verses apply to your own life?

Is the transformational process a joint-partnership between you and the Spirit? Or does God do it on His own? If it is joint, what is your part to play?

3. Being transformed by the Spirit causes you to become more like Christ. Romans 8:29 states it like this: "For those whom He foreknew, He also predestined to become conformed to the image of His Son, so that He would be the firstborn among many brethren."

What does it mean to be "conformed to the image of His Son" in everyday practical examples?

The "fruit of the Spirit" are qualities of Jesus Christ made manifest through the Spirit's work of transformation in your life. These are listed in Galatians 5:22-23. In the line beside each quality below, rank yourself from 1 to 10, with 10 being the most, on how you feel you're reflecting Jesus in these areas.

Love _____

Joy _____

Peace _____

Patience _____

Kindness _____

Goodness _____

Faithfulness _____

Gentleness _____

Self-control _____

Share which top three qualities come most naturally to you and why you think that is.

Now look at your lowest two qualities. Will you commit to regularly asking God for growth in these two areas? What is something practical you can do to help increase your growth in these two areas?

4. Read together what David wrote in Psalm 51:11: "Do not cast me away from Your presence and do not take Your Holy Spirit from me."

This verse gives us a glimpse into how valuable David, the man after God's own heart, considered the Holy Spirit's presence in his life. What does this reveal to you about David's dependence on the Spirit to live the life God had called him to?

Why is it important to stay authentic and honest in our relationship with the Holy Spirit as we seek to grow spiritually?

What often happens when we seek to do things on our own and ignore the need for the transformative presence of the Spirit with us each moment? What has happened to you?

5. To be transformed is not a passive action that occurs to you. You don't just sit back and the transformation takes place. For the infection of your soul to be addressed, you must first come to God with an unveiled face and then come to the mirror of His written Word, the Bible. You must position that mirror so that the light of God's Spirit shines on it, revealing to you the truth you need for personal transformation. When you hear this truth, you are then to apply it.

Read together James 1:19-21:

This you know, my beloved brethren. But everyone must be quick to hear, slow to speak and slow to anger; for the anger of man does not achieve the righteousness of God. Therefore, putting aside all filthiness and all that remains of wickedness, in humility receive the word implanted, which is able to save your souls.

James was writing to believers who were already saved for eternity, and the word translated from the original language as "save" here means "to sanctify." How does the Word of God sanctify a person's soul?

What is an active, participatory step believers can take to increase this sanctification process?

In Closing

As you end the session today, pray together for a greater work within you of the Spirit's transformational process. Ask the Spirit for the courage to allow Him to take the mess and garbage of your life and apply His work to it in order to produce growth and something good.

Before session 3, complete the "On Your Own Between Sessions" section below. You might want to start the next session with willing participants sharing what they learned from the exercises on the following pages.

On Your Own Between Sessions

1. Read the following verses below and on page 28:

   Romans 12:2 — "Do not be conformed to this world, but be transformed by the renewing of your mind, so that you may prove what the will of God is, that which is good and acceptable and perfect."

   Philippians 1:6 — "For I am confident of this very thing, that He who began a good work in you will perfect it until the day of Christ Jesus."

Titus 3:5 — "He saved us, not on the basis of deeds which we have done in righteousness, but according to His mercy, by the washing of regeneration and renewing by the Holy Spirit."

What do these verses tell you about the intended goal of the Spirit's transformative work in your life?

List three distinct principles about the Lord's work as relayed in these verses.

    1.

    2.

    3.

2. Let's consider the reasons (emotions and convictions) you may have for holding on to your old ways and qualities rather than being transformed to be like the Lord Jesus Christ. Then contrast those reasons with the benefits you might gain by pursuing becoming more like Him.

Reasons for Retaining Your Old Ways	Benefits of Becoming More Like Christ
*	*
*	*
*	*
*	*
*	*

3. Chapter 5 in *The Power of the Holy Spirit's Names* book reminds us that knowing the Holy Spirit according to the name *Lord* brings about a change in our surrender to Him as well as to the governing Word of God. Tony writes,

The mirror brings reality into focus for you. It shows you what's wrong. It shows you what needs to adjust. It shows you what is real, like mirrors are designed to do. When you approach the Word of God as a mirror for the Spirit to use in your life, you're no longer just reading a page. You're reading about your own personality exposed in the Word. The Spirit of the Lord brings you freedom from bondage and deliverance from spiritual death by illuminating the Word in your spirit, which then nourishes your soul and positively affects your body.

We are not to live as hearers of the Word only. Each of us must be an effectual doer. Just as the term *Lord* is given to someone who typically governs another, the Word is to govern our spirits within. The Word is to influence what actions we take. The Word promotes and produces growth as we gaze into it and abide in it through the power of the Spirit.

The Power of the Holy Spirit's Names, pages 89-90

Consider some unhealthy thought patterns or beliefs you may have about God's Word and any reluctance you may have toward it fully governing your life. List two that you would like to surrender to God and ask Him to remove, change, replace, or transform them.

1.

2.

Take some time to pray through these two items (or as many as you want) and invite the Holy Spirit to go to work within you in order to bring about a greater level of trust and respect for the Word of God.

What do you hope to gain as you grow in your relationship with the Holy Spirit as well as in your understanding and application of the Word of God?

4. Life Experiment: Meditate Daily

This week, read the following excerpt from the book *The Power of the Holy Spirit's Names* book once or twice daily. Meditate on different aspects of the concept in it each day, then write down your thoughts in response.

> If you're not changing or maturing spiritually in your walk with the Spirit, you're either not coming to God with an unveiled, honest face or not allowing the Word to mirror your own life and reveal it. When you're able to do both of those things consistently, the changes take place internally. The Spirit of the Lord frees you up to live more like Christ in your actions, attitudes, character, and conduct. You begin to resemble Jesus as you go through your life.
>
> After all, that's the Spirit's goal. He's been given to us so we may glorify Christ. The Holy Spirit abides in us so we might know what it means to truly surrender to the Lord of lords and King of kings in all we think, say, and do. You will progressively be transformed from glory to glory, that is, from one level of spiritual development to the next. You will be set free to be everything you were designed to be.
>
> When a woman is pregnant, it shows. Her appetite changes. Her mood changes. Her body changes. It shows because life is growing on the inside. When you receive the Word implanted within you, when you abide and allow it to do its work in you, it will also show. What you choose to do for entertainment will change. What you say will change. Even your emotions and your mood will change. Everything will change because of the new life growing on the inside.
>
> And just as a woman relies on physical intimacy to create the new life within her, the Holy Spirit relies on spiritual intimacy to do the same. It's in the closeness and authenticity of your relationship with the Spirit of the Lord that the liberty you've been desiring all this time will grow within you. The Holy Spirit entered you at the conception of your salvation. But for the Spirit to grow within, you need to hang out with and be intimate with the Word of God in such a way that it reveals you to you and produces the spiritual growth you need and desire.
>
> *The Power of the Holy Spirit's Names*, page 90

Consider sharing the thoughts you wrote down when you gather for the next session.

Recommended Reading

In preparation for session 3, please read chapter 6 of *The Power of the Holy Spirit's Names* book.

THE WINE

The following is an excerpt from *The Power of the Holy Spirit's Names* book, focusing on the Holy Spirit as the Wine.

Being filled with the Spirit is not something you do; it's something you allow to be done to you. You have as much access to the Holy Spirit's filling as I do. The more believers in a church who constantly operate with the filling of the Spirit, the stronger that church will be. The fewer operating with the Spirit's filling, the weaker that church will be.

We all have equal access to the Spirit. What's more, as we see with Paul's using the present tense of the term *fill*, we are to allow this filling to be an ongoing part of every moment. It's not something you do once and are done with it. Just like you wouldn't fill up your car with gas or charge it with electricity once and be done with it. You can't live on yesterday's filling of the Holy Spirit. What you got yesterday was meant for yesterday. The Holy Spirit is to fill you each and every day.

You may know Christians who like to talk about what God did for them yesterday, or even a few months or years ago. Sometimes even decades ago. It's almost as if God hasn't done anything for them lately. When testimonies of God's work in someone's life speak only of the past, you have to wonder if that person has fallen back asleep in their spiritual walk.

The Holy Spirit is a present participant in life's realities. Just like a car needs more fuel to keep going—or a person needs more alcohol to once more be drunk again—the filling of the Holy Spirit doesn't happen just once. It's an ongoing filling you allow to happen to you on a regular basis.

Most of us probably know what it's like to walk away from a church service or a spiritual event and feel full of the Holy Spirit. Somehow, our being together with others focused on God allows the Spirit to fill those who are open to Him even more. The atmosphere in these situations is often thick with the presence of God.

But then we also probably know what it's like to reach the parking lot after one of these services or events only to feel that the presence of the Spirit is dissipating. As we get into our car and hear the noises all around us, or strike up a conversation with our spouse, or turn on the radio to listen to the news, or even slip into traffic, we can literally feel it eroding and escaping. We no longer feel as spiritual as we did just minutes before inside the building's doors. While we said "Amen" and "Hallelujah" in the service, those words are nowhere near our lips now. Frustration even creeps in—as well as disappointment.

Like when a car leaves a gas station, the fuel has begun to burn away.

Unfortunately, far too many people rely on the filling to take place at a church service or somewhere else external they can plug into. But if that isn't happening 24/7, you won't be in much of a good spot when it comes to living out your life.

The Power of the Holy Spirit's Names, pages 100-102

Video Teaching Notes

As you watch the video, use the space below to take notes. Some key points and quotes are provided as reminders.

Main Idea

- Like wine can control our bodies, the Spirit has the power to control our thoughts and behaviors. To wake up and influence the world for God, we must listen to the Spirit and let Him lead us. How easily is the Spirit's influence on our lives visible to others?

- We must learn to see the world from God's perspective so we fulfill His purposes, and we do that through the pervading influence of the Holy Spirit.

- To be filled with the Spirit is to:

  » release control of yourself to Him (Luke 4:1-2).

  » be awake, not sleepwalking, through our calling to live like Jesus.

  » discern God's leading in our lives.

- The filling of the Spirit is ongoing, like filling a gas tank repeatedly to keep the car running, and we do it by prioritizing God's Word, the act of worship, and the mindset of gratitude throughout our days.

- Personal Notes:

Application

Seek (and do so regularly) God's leading by asking Him to bring you into alignment with His will through the influence of the Holy Spirit. Then find one specific way to serve or minister to others this week.

Quotables

- God wants believers to learn how to operate under spiritual influence, dominated by the Spirit's work that has been deposited into the life of every believer.

- The moment that we stop pulling over to the filling station of the Holy Spirit, we stall in our spiritual life like a car stalls when it runs out of gas.

- When you are full of self…then there is no room for God…When you are full of self, you block the work of the Holy Spirit.

Video Group Discussion

1. In the video session, Tony compares the similarities between being drunk with wine and being filled with the Spirit. Whether or not you've ever personally been drunk, you've undoubtedly seen someone drunk in real life or being portrayed as drunk on television or in a film. What happens to a person's cognitive thoughts as well as bodily functions when they're drunk with wine?

   In what way is this a good illustration for how much we are to yield our thoughts and life to the Holy Spirit?

2. What part of the video teaching stood out to you the most? Tell why this principle resonated with you as well as how it made you feel.

3. Tony said the believer's role in being filled with the Holy Spirit is in many ways passive. The Holy Spirit will fill us if we make room. What are some of the things that could get in the way and crowd out the room needed for the Spirit to inhabit and fill us fully?

   How can we address the removal of these hindrances to the filling of the Holy Spirit? What are some practical steps we can take to remove the distractions and open ourselves more to the Spirit's filling?

4. Tony closed the video session by talking about the difference between "going to worship service" and "living a life of worship." He explained that many people mistakenly believe that worship is an activity or an event. But in order to be full of the Holy Spirit, worship must be a lifestyle. What are three tangible steps people can take to integrate a lifestyle of worship into their days on a regular basis?

   1.

   2.

   3.

   How crucial is it to make room for the Holy Spirit throughout your day? Will He ever seek to abide where He isn't welcomed and allowed? Why or why not?

Group Bible Exploration

1. Read together Ephesians 5:15-21:

   > Be careful how you walk, not as unwise men but as wise, making the most of your time, because the days are evil. So then do not be foolish, but understand what the will of the Lord is. And do not get drunk with wine, for that is dissipation, but be filled with the Spirit, speaking to one another in psalms and hymns and spiritual songs, singing and making melody with your heart to the Lord; always giving thanks for all things in the name of our Lord Jesus Christ to God, even the Father; and be subject to one another in the fear of Christ.

   Explain the connection between being filled with the Holy Spirit and psalms, hymns, and spiritual songs.

   Can a believer be filled with the Holy Spirit while living in a constant state of grumbling and complaint? Why or why not?

   How crucial is it to "be subject to one another in the fear of Christ" in order to fully live out and experience "what the will of the Lord is" in your life? Explain why you chose to answer as you did.

   What does this principle of being subject to one another say about the biblical concept of "unity"?

2. Read together Colossians 3:16:

> Let the word of Christ richly dwell within you, with all wisdom teaching and admonishing one another with psalms and hymns and spiritual songs, singing with thankfulness in your hearts to God.

Describe the correlation and similarities between this verse in Colossians with the passage we read in Ephesians 5:15-21 on page 35.

In what practical ways ought being filled by the Spirit show up in what we choose to dwell on with our thoughts as well as in what we say and do?

3. In both these passages, the key to the filling of the Holy Spirit is worship. Read the following verses and identify key takeaways for how to worship effectively or about what the power of worship can do in a person's life.

> John 4:24 — "God is spirit, and those who worship Him must worship in spirit and truth."

> Job 1:20-21 — "Then Job arose and tore his robe and shaved his head, and he fell to the ground and worshiped. He said, 'Naked I came from my mother's womb, and naked I shall return there. The Lord gave and the Lord has taken away. Blessed be the name of the Lord.'"

> Matthew 4:10 — "Then Jesus said to him, 'Go, Satan! For it is written, "You shall worship the Lord your God, and serve Him only."'"

In Closing

As you end the study today, pray together for a greater filling of the Holy Spirit in each of your lives. Ask God to revive or restore your worship life.

Before session 4, complete the "On Your Own Between Sessions" section below.

On Your Own Between Sessions

1. Chapter 6 in *The Power of the Holy Spirit's Names* book says,

   > Paul compares what happens when a person drinks too much wine to what can happen when we're filled by the Spirit. He encourages each of us to become spiritually full or intoxicated by the Spirit rather than becoming full or intoxicated from alcohol.
   >
   > When you and I become full of the Holy Spirit, He is free to influence our thoughts and behavior.

   > *The Power of the Holy Spirit's Names*, page 96

   Tony then goes on to say,

   > The filling of the Spirit is designed to produce discernable behavioral differences.
   >
   > Filled with the Spirit, your views ought to be different. Your standards ought to be different. Your words definitely ought to be different. Even your courage to carry out God's will ought to be different.

   > *The Power of the Holy Spirit's Names*, page 97

   What does it mean to have the Spirit free to "influence our thoughts and behavior"?

   Have you ever moved ahead on something you didn't feel you had the courage to do on your own because the Holy Spirit gave you the boldness you needed? What did you learn from that experience? If your answer was no, identify an area where you could use some extra courage, and then ask the Spirit to provide it.

What specific step can you take to align your views, standards, and thoughts more with God's will and allow the Holy Spirit to influence you even more than He does now?

2. Read Romans 5:3-5:

> Not only this, but we also exult in our tribulations, knowing that tribulation brings about perseverance; and perseverance, proven character; and proven character, hope; and hope does not disappoint, because the love of God has been poured out within our hearts through the Holy Spirit who was given to us.

What's one way the Holy Spirit helps us during difficulties?

What hesitations toward hope pop up in you when you face trials?

How can a deeper abiding with the Holy Spirit nurture a more solid and reliable hope in you?

3. Read 1 Corinthians 6:19:

> Do you not know that your body is a temple of the Holy Spirit who is in you, whom you have from God, and that you are not your own?

What is the implied meaning behind your body being the temple of the Spirit?

How does it make you feel to realize you are "not your own"?

What does this verse reveal regarding God's level of love and responsibility toward you? Consider how "ownership" often increases the level of care and responsibility in every-day life situations and belongings and how that may translate to God's interaction and care with you.

4. In chapter 6 of *The Power of the Holy Spirit's Names* book, Tony mentioned,

> Make no mistake, we live in an evil world. Evil surrounds us on every corner. Jesus defeated Satan at the cross, but Satan has still been given a long leash from which to operate on earth until Jesus' final return. To say that Satan has made the most of that leash is an understatement. Much to the detriment of so many worldwide, he's put on a party.
>
> We don't have time to lie around in our perpetual states of ease. Instead, we must do what Paul urged next: "So then do not be foolish, but understand what the will of the Lord is" (Ephesians 5:17). We must understand what God's will is so we can enact it. We must learn how to look at life from God's perspective so we're fulfilling His purposes not only in our individual lives but also as a Christian col-lective. God desires to work both in and through us for the betterment of others and the advancement of His kingdom agenda on earth.
>
> But we can't do that until we wake up.
>
> *The Power of the Holy Spirit's Names*, pages 95-96

Identify three areas in your life you can upgrade from "time-wasters" to "kingdom-investors."

1.

2.

3.

Pray for insight on how to take steps in these three areas in order to better utilize them for the advancement of God's kingdom agenda on earth.

5. Life Exercise: Participating in Your Own Advancement in Being Used to Make an Impact

Identify one area or person in your sphere of influence where spiritual impact would be welcomed and needed.

Consider how to approach the situation through abiding in the Holy Spirit and asking Him to open the doors for you as well as to give you wisdom on what to say or do to make a positive impact.

Evaluate how to move forward in measurable ways once you've discerned the Spirit's direction.

Share if you feel led. After you've stepped out underneath the Spirit's leading and influence in your own life in order to positively impact someone else's life, take a moment to assess and mentally process what took place. This specific "Life Exercise" may take more than a week to fully experience, but consider sharing with the group when the results are in — or even after the study is over.

Recommended Reading

In preparation for session 4, please read chapters 7–8 of *The Power of the Holy Spirit's Names* book.

THE INTERCESSOR

The following is an excerpt from *The Power of the Holy Spirit's Names* book, focusing on the Holy Spirit as the Intercessor.

Even if only through films or TV dramas, we all know the pain associated with childbirth is real. Yet the groans of a woman in labor, which sound like bad news, signal a good situation. Childbirth hurts, yes, but it's because someone new is about to be born.

Now, I get it. The fact that someone new is being birthed doesn't negate the pain of the process. But neither is the pain of the process limited to pain. The pain exists to produce a greater joy and reality.

This reality for all of us is that life hurts. Its difficulties, traumas, and hidden troubles come to us—and often at the most inopportune times. We'd all love a life with no pain, anguish, or sorrow, but if you've lived long enough to know, you know that isn't an option. Again, life hurts. And as I've become all too familiar with recently, at times circumstances and loss both affect you and infect you to such a degree that all you can do is groan.

Have you ever been there? Do you know what it's like to run out of words to explain what you're going through? Have you experienced those seasons when you don't even have the strength to pray anymore? At one point or another, most of us have. Which is why God has given us this next name of the Holy Spirit. In Romans 8, we pick up looking at Paul's struggle between the flesh and the spirit, and as we do, we come across a most powerful and needed character attribute and role of the Holy Spirit. He is the Intercessor.

An intercessor appeals to someone on behalf of a situation or another person. They are a go-between, like lawyers who plead their clients' cases before a judge or jury. They intercede in situations that are due to troubles or difficulties. And Romans 8 tells us we have an intercessor when life causes us to groan. We have a representative when we face suffering. In short, we have hope.

Suffering is the pain of negative circumstances or even unmet expectations. When this pain hits you so hard that it overwhelms you, you need someone else to lend a helping hand.

The Power of the Holy Spirit's Names, pages 125-126

Video Teaching Notes

As you watch the video, use the space below to take notes. Some key points and quotes are provided as reminders.

Main Idea

- Life hurts, and often we don't even have the words to express our pain. In a world of suffering, the Holy Spirit is our go-between with God, a source of strength for us if we allow ourselves to see our circumstances through God's view.

- Suffering reminds us that this world is not all there is. It forces us to remember God and see life through a spiritual perspective (Romans 8:22-28).

- Sometimes we hurt so much that we don't know what to say or even have the energy to say it when we pray. And pain distorts our view of reality. It also often draws our attention only to itself. But the Spirit intercedes for us. He knows our hearts and our desires intimately. Like an ASL (American Sign Language) interpreter, the Spirit takes our heart cry to the Father with accurate interpretation of our need.

- God uses suffering to conform us to His image, to encourage us to trust in Him, and to develop an eternal perspective in us (2 Corinthians 1:3-10). It's always better to hope in God rather than in ourselves.

- Personal Notes:

Application

During difficult times, remember that the Spirit is praying for you. Listen carefully through prayer for His leading, and allow Him to comfort you with His presence.

Quotables

- It is the Holy Spirit's job to meet us in the groans of life in order to sustain us as we walk through life to give birth to the new life that is to come.

- The word *intercession* is an interventionist. It's like a help desk that intervenes in order to sustain us during groaning times.

- Providence is the mysterious way in which God intervenes and connects people, places, and things at the right time to meet you when you're hurting the most.

Video Group Discussion

1. Read together Romans 8:22-23:

   We know that the whole creation groans and suffers the pains of childbirth together until now. And not only this, but also we ourselves, having the first fruits of the Spirit, even we ourselves groan within ourselves, waiting eagerly for our adoption as sons, the redemption of our body.

   What does the phrase "redemption of our body" mean to you personally?

   Describe some of the difficulties we face living in finite bodies bound by time.

   What are some coping mechanisms people adopt to deal with the reality of the frailties in our human bodies? Can coping mechanisms ever become an idol or distraction from God? If your answer is yes, why do you feel that way?

2. Read together Romans 8:26-27:

> In the same way the Spirit also helps our weakness; for we do not know how to pray as we should, but the Spirit Himself intercedes for us with groanings too deep for words; and He who searches the hearts knows what the mind of the Spirit is, because He intercedes for the saints according to the will of God.

Describe a situation or need where you weren't able to pray as you had hoped or would have liked. What did you learn from this experience?

Do you believe the Holy Spirit intercedes for you in times of great need, even if you don't see Him doing it? Why or why not?

Have you ever come to the point where you asked the Holy Spirit to pray for you? Share as much about that situation as you feel comfortable doing. Did you experience any healing or hope after you turned to the Spirit to pray on your behalf?

3. In the video, Tony explained how Jesus and the Holy Spirit work together to intercede on our behalf. He said,

> The Bible declares in Hebrews 7:25 that Jesus is our intercessor. How does that work with the Holy Spirit? Well, Jesus intercedes for us from heaven. The Holy Spirit brings that heavenly intercession to us. We have a head, then we have the body, but between the head and the body is the neck, and that neck links the head with the body. We are the body of Christ. Jesus is the head of the body. The Holy

Spirit is like the neck to attach the intercessory work of Jesus with the needs of the body, particularly during times of weakness.

How does the truth that Jesus and the Spirit work together to intercede for you affect you emotionally?

4. During the video, Tony shared about a personal time of need. He talked about heading out on his first trip for a Bible study filming since his wife's passing due to cancer, just a few months earlier. She had usually accompanied him on these trips. That made it even harder, and as he walked the corridors of the airport, he felt down and depressed. But then the Lord sent him a couple who recognized him from the TV broadcast and asked if they could pray for him. Tony reminded us that God "providentially" arranges people and places to meet us where we need His loving hand. This is an example of Romans 8:28, where God takes a difficult situation and produces good in and through it.

Read together Romans 8:28:

> We know that God causes all things to work together for good to those who love God, to those who are called according to His purpose.

Discuss the process of how God can work all things together for good.

What are some hindrances against or qualifications for God working all things together for good?

Has God ever shown up through a person, a song, a sermon, or an event when you needed Him at a low point in your life, like He did for Tony at the airport? Can you share about what you learned through that experience? If you don't think God has ever done this for you, what can you learn from His doing it for others—again, like He did in Tony's situation?

5. Tony concluded the video teaching by referring to James 1, which talks about how God can use the trials and difficulties of life to bring about spiritual maturity and completion in our growth (James 1:1-4). What resonates most with you from that principle?

Group Bible Exploration

1. Read together Romans 8:5-8:

> Those who are according to the flesh set their minds on the things of the flesh, but those who are according to the Spirit, the things of the Spirit. For the mind set on the flesh is death, but the mind set on the Spirit is life and peace, because the mind set on the flesh is hostile toward God; for it does not subject itself to the law of God, for it is not even able to do so, and those who are in the flesh cannot please God.

Based on this passage, what are some of the major differences between setting your mind on the flesh versus setting your mind on the Spirit?

What does it mean—in a practical, day-by-day experience—to set your mind on the Spirit?

2. Now read together 1 Corinthians 2:10-12:

> To us God revealed them through the Spirit; for the Spirit searches all things, even the depths of God. For who among men knows the thoughts of a man except the spirit of the man which is in him? Even so the thoughts of God no one knows except the Spirit of God. Now we have received, not the spirit of the world, but the Spirit who is from God, so that we may know the things freely given to us by God.

In what ways does the Holy Spirit's knowledge of our needs (Romans 8:26-27) combined with His knowledge of the "depths of God" help Him in His role as an intercessor?

Tony compared the Spirit's intercession work in chapter 8 of *The Power of the Holy Spirit's Names* book to that of a translator of ASL, serving as a go-between for people to understand what they could not previously understand. In what ways does the Holy Spirit need to translate our needs to God?

In what ways does the Holy Spirit need to translate God's responses and will to us?

Do you think you can experience the full effect of the Spirit's translation of God's will to your heart without an authentic, abiding relationship with the Spirit? Why or why not?

3. Read together 1 John 5:14-15:

> This is the confidence which we have before Him, that, if we ask anything according to His will, He hears us. And if we know that He hears us in whatever we ask, we know that we have the requests which we have asked from Him.

The Bible connects asking and receiving with doing so in accordance with God's will. Describe how the Holy Spirit intercedes in our hearts to interpret and explain God's will to us throughout our various experiences.

What can you do to personally open your heart more to hearing from the Spirit?

4. Based on Isaiah 29:13-15 below, how does God feel about hearts that are closed off to Him or far away from Him?

> The Lord said, "Because this people draw near with their words and honor Me with their lip service, but they remove their hearts far from Me, and their reverence for Me consists of tradition learned by rote, therefore behold, I will once again deal marvelously with this people, wondrously marvelous; and the wisdom of their wise men will perish, and the discernment of their discerning men will be concealed." Woe to those who deeply hide their plans from the LORD, and whose deeds are done in a dark place, and they say, "Who sees us?" or "Who knows us?"

What does it mean to draw near to God with all of your heart? Provide a practical example of what that could look like in your daily life.

On a scale of 1 to 10, where would you rate how your heart is open or closed to God (1 being least, 10 being most)?

1 --- 10

Now on a scale of 1 to 10, where would you rate your felt level of the Spirit's interceding on your behalf, both in going to God in prayer for you and also in guiding you according to God's will (again, 1 being least, 10 being most)?

1 --- 10

Do you see any correlation between the two graphs? Explain.

As Tony writes in *The Power of the Holy Spirit's Names* book, "God isn't interested in empty words. He wants to hear what our heart is saying when we cry out to Him" (page 133). The Holy Spirit's role is to help us connect with God on a more authentic and honest, heartfelt level. When we do, we receive an abundance of answered prayer, clarity, and comfort when we need it most. And isn't that what we're really hoping for? We want to place an online order for "instant relief." Tony goes on to say on that page, "But we won't get the relief we need until we learn how to pray according to God's will"—and with a heart after His own.

In Closing

As you close today's time together, encourage one another to pursue closeness with God through abiding in His Spirit. Talk about ways you can prioritize your relationship with the Lord and even hold one another accountable to pursue Him at the level you'd like to. Spend a few minutes in prayer together, asking the Spirit to reveal God's will to each of you and to the group in relation to how you can all grow more deeply spiritually and leave an impact for Christ wherever you go.

Before session 5, complete the "On Your Own Between Sessions" section below.

On Your Own Between Sessions

1. Read 2 Corinthians 1:8-10 on page 50:

We do not want you to be unaware, brethren, of our affliction which came to us in Asia, that we were burdened excessively, beyond our strength, so that we despaired even of life; indeed, we had the sentence of death within ourselves so that we would not trust in ourselves, but in God who raises the dead; who delivered us from so great a peril of death, and will deliver us, He on whom we have set our hope. And He will yet deliver us.

What does this passage teach us about a committed saint's capacity to become depressed, down, or in despair? Keep in mind that Paul wrote this passage.

Have you ever been so down that you "despaired even of life," like Paul did? What did you learn through that experience?

Describe the difference between despairing apart from a hope in God and going through despair while placing your hope on God. In what ways can you increase your dependence on Him during times of trial, and how can the Holy Spirit take a more active role in this process with you?

2. In chapter 8 of *The Power of the Holy Spirit's Names* book, Tony writes,

I hope Paul's transparency will help you have greater courage. I hope his despair lifts your spirit some, if only in that you know you are not alone. You aren't the only one who's reached the point of wanting to quit, give up, or throw in the towel. When life crashes in on you and you feel oppressed from every side, take comfort in realizing that others have also walked this path. Others have clung to the walls of the pit unsure if they should keep climbing or just let go.

The apostle Paul is one of them. So if he can hit rock bottom, anyone can. Spiritual people can, and do, hit rock bottom. We are human. And life does hurt.

The Power of the Holy Spirit's Names, page 130

Summarize the following three Scriptures in your own words, mindful to apply the principles in them to you personally.

Matthew 5:4 — "Blessed are those who mourn, for they shall be comforted."

Psalm 119:50 — "This is my comfort in my affliction, that Your word has revived me."

Psalm 34:18 — "The Lord is near to the brokenhearted and saves those who are crushed in spirit."

3. In chapter 8 of *The Power of the Holy Spirit's Names* book, Tony writes,

> I wish I could tell you that life won't collapse and the walls won't feel as if they're caving in. I wish I could say that will be true for you. But as I know from my own experience, life does collapse, and when it does, it crashes down hard. Sometimes all at once…But I can tell you that when the world crashes in on you, you have Someone who will show up as an intercessor when you need Him the most. The Holy Spirit will pray for you when you don't have the words to pray for yourself. He will take your inarticulate expressions of anguish and turn them into a powerful prayer to God.
>
> *The Power of the Holy Spirit's Names,* page 131

In what way does honesty and truthfulness about your emotions allow the Spirit to do God's work in your life?

In our "positive vibes only" culture, is it ever difficult to be transparent, even with yourself, about how difficult things are or how low you may be feeling? Explain why you answered the way you did.

Does reading about how honest Paul was during his low points give you encouragement to be more honest with God? Why or why not?

4. Life Exercise: Discover Comfort When You Need It Most

This week, make a point to be honest with God about how you're feeling. It's okay to tell Him the truth. After all, He already knows. If you have pain from your past or bruises in your present, talk to Him about it. Let Him know you're open to receiving His interceding presence and power of the Holy Spirit.

Spend some time thinking through the principles we studied together this week. This was a deep lesson dealing with our hurts and wounds. Allow God's Word and the truth of the Holy Spirit's desire to comfort you become real for you more and more each day. Ask the Spirit to intercede for you in the areas you need it most. In fact, ask Him to reveal areas where you need comfort that may have been pushed to the side because it felt too hard to deal with them on your own.

As you continually seek the Spirit's intercession in your life, let Him know you're grateful for the work He's doing in you. Remember the principles from earlier lessons, and spend time singing or worshipping with a heart of thankfulness so that the Spirit feels all the more at home in your heart.

Recommended Reading

In preparation for session 5, read chapter 9 of *The Power of the Holy Spirit's Names* book.

THE SEAL

The following is an excerpt from *The Power of the Holy Spirit's Names* book, focusing on the Holy Spirit as the Seal.

We often get confused about what are the real problems in life and what are merely illusions of problems. This is because without tapping into the Holy Spirit's insight, we rely on our own spiritual eyes, which are darkened. When you fail to see things spiritually, you react to things physically. When you fail to trust in God's sovereignty, your body reacts with anxiety. When you fail to step out in faith, you backtrack in fear.

To perceive things spiritually and apply God's truth to that which you perceive is a gift of the Spirit's seal in your life…

You and I can live in the physical according to our physical senses. We are given free will. If we want to remain autonomous, God gives us that choice. But if we do make that choice, we'll also be choosing to live life apart from spiritual enlightenment. Our choices and emotions will no doubt reflect this reality. Only when we allow all of the elements of the seal of the Holy Spirit to be fully expressed in our life will we tap into all of the benefits the Spirit is designed to supply.

Psalm 103:7 distinguishes between those who choose to walk in the physical and those who choose to walk in the spiritual: "He made known His ways to Moses, His acts to the sons of Israel." Moses saw the ways of God while Israel got to see only His acts.

To put it another way, Israel saw what God did. Moses saw who God is. He saw the why and the how behind what God did. He got more information than that of an observer. He was a participant in the mighty acts of God Himself.

So really, it depends on what you want out of life. Do you want to sit on the sidelines and watch what God does for other people? Or do you want to walk up the mountain to experience God, like Moses did, face-to-face? Do you want to be in the crowd, or do you want insider information? It really is your choice. God will never force you to walk according to His ways. But He will enable you to do so through the sealing of the Holy Spirit. What you do with His gift is entirely up to you…

When you discover how to walk according to the illumination of spiritual eyes, you'll discover a life you only dreamed of before. Look all throughout the Bible for examples of this.

Joshua would normally have relied on a proven military strategy for taking on the city of Jericho, but God told him to have his men march around the city in order to make the walls fall down. That's not a great strategy, if you ask me. But it worked because it was God's method for winning that battle.

Gideon probably wanted all thirty thousand of his men to go in and fight a battle in order to give him the odds he felt were comfortable enough to enter the war at all. But God instructed him to use three hundred men instead. Gideon was able to obey God because he understood the difference between the spiritual and the physical.

Another example is Abraham. Abraham never would have come up with the idea of offering his son Isaac on that altar in hopes that God would somehow intervene at the last minute, offering instead a ram. But that's what God asked him to do, and he did it. As a result, Abraham continued to experience the full manifestation of the power of God in his life to do great things and be the father of many nations…

God longs to work experientially in your life through the indwelling of the Holy Spirit. When that takes place, you'll see Him start showing up for you in ways you never anticipated. You'll get to see God's hand in your life moving and shifting things for you, opening doors you, again, didn't even know to knock on. This is because God sees all things. You and I see only what we can with our physical eyes. But when we learn to tap into the enlightenment of the Holy Spirit, we learn to see things spiritually.

The Power of the Holy Spirit's Names, pages 148-150

Video Teaching Notes

As you watch the video, use the space below to take notes. Some key points and quotes are provided as reminders.

Main Idea

- The permanent presence through the indwelling of the Holy Spirit guarantees our security, establishes His ownership, and radiates the power of His authority throughout our lives.

- We are "sealed with the Spirit" once for all. Our salvation is permanent (Ephesians 1:13-14; 4:30; Romans 8:35-39).

- We belong to Jesus because of the cross, thus making us stewards, not owners, of the lives we live (1 Corinthians 6:19-20).

- God authorizes us to draw on the power of the Spirit in our lives—enlightening us, strengthening us, going before us.

- The Spirit in us now is a down payment of our eternal security with God.

- Personal Notes:

Application

The Spirit's work in your life now assures you of your eternal future with Him. Spend time thanking Him for His presence and work in your daily life. Ask Him to help you make decisions with the eternal future in mind.

Quotables

- God has sealed us with the Holy Spirit. He has integrated His Spirit with our spirit so that there is a permanent relationship with God.

- Growing in your walk with the Holy Spirit is critical to looking forward to the day of redemption.

- When the Holy Spirit…sees that you are reflecting His heart in your relationships, then you will feel His satisfaction with you as He ministers grace to you while you minister grace to others.

Video Group Discussion

1. Tony opens the teaching on the sealing of the Holy Spirit by referring to the Spirit as "Christ in you." He then goes on to share that the Spirit begins a remodeling project within your soul. What are some areas that commonly need to be remodeled in people's souls?

In what ways can a person cooperate more intentionally with this internal remodeling job?

2. Read Ephesians 1:13-14:

> In Him, you also, after listening to the message of truth, the gospel of your salvation—having also believed, you were sealed in Him with the Holy Spirit of promise, who is given as a pledge of our inheritance, with a view to the redemption of God's own possession, to the praise of His glory.

What do these verses reveal about the purpose of the Holy Spirit's sealing work in our lives?

3. In the video, Tony compared the permanent residing of God with us through the sealing of the Spirit to pouring cream into coffee. Once the cream is poured in, it permanently becomes one with the coffee. Tony said, "When I'm drinking my coffee now, I cannot extract the cream out because the coffee has been sealed with the presence of the cream, because it is becoming a permanent transformational environment in which my coffee operates, which changes and adjusts the taste."

In what ways does the sealing of the Spirit provide a "transformational environment" in believers' lives?

When cream and coffee merge, it forms a permanent, bonded seal. Tony used this example to illustrate the permanency of our seal of the Spirit to indicate how intertwined we become. Describe the difference between relationships based on the unknown elements of potential eventual separation and those based on a bonded seal such as with family or marriage.

In what ways does the bonded seal allow you to rest more fully in God's acceptance of you?

4. In the video, Tony mentioned that the seal of the Spirit can be compared to a woman wearing an engagement ring. Her behavior changes based on that ring. She no longer considers herself at liberty to date anyone she wants. The ring is a promise of things to come. The Holy Spirit's presence in our lives is to serve as a constant reminder of the great expectations we have for eternity. Reflect on the following passages and talk about what eternity means to each of you.

Colossians 3:2 — "Set your mind on the things above, not on the things that are on earth."

2 Corinthians 4:18 — "We look not at the things which are seen, but at the things which are not seen; for the things which are seen are temporal, but the things which are not seen are eternal."

Matthew 13:43 — "The righteous will shine forth as the sun in the kingdom of their Father. He who has ears, let him hear."

Now pray as a group, asking the Spirit to make you more aware of the treasures to come in eternity. Ask Him to place in you an ever-growing hope toward that time so that you can rest in the loving security of His presence while living your life on earth.

Group Bible Exploration

1. In chapter 9 of *The Power of the Holy Spirit's Names* book, Tony explains that the "seal of the Spirit" represents three distinct areas:

Three concepts are tied to this specific name of the sealing presence of the Spirit. The first concept is that it guarantees security. The second concept is that it establishes ownership. And the third is that it's reflective of authority. Thus the Seal outlines that which pertains to our security, ownership, and authorization.

The Power of the Holy Spirit's Names, page 140

Read the following verses, then circle which of the three concepts Tony identifies (security, ownership, authority) each one most relates to and share why you chose the concepts you did. The verses may not use the word *seal* expressly, but they do relate to one of the three concepts the "seal of the Spirit" brings about in a believer's life.

Ephesians 4:30 — "Do not grieve the Holy Spirit of God, by whom you were sealed for the day of redemption."

Security

Ownership

Authority

Esther 8:8 — "You write to the Jews as you see fit, in the king's name, and seal it with the king's signet ring; for a decree which is written in the name of the king and sealed with the king's signet ring may not be revoked."

Security

Ownership

Authority

Jeremiah 32:9-10 — "I bought the field which was at Anathoth from Hanamel my uncle's son, and I weighed out the silver for him, seventeen shekels of silver. I signed and sealed the deed, and called in witnesses, and weighed out the silver on the scales."

Security

Ownership

Authority

Daniel 6:17 — "A stone was brought and laid over the mouth of the den; and the king sealed it with his own signet ring and with the signet rings of his nobles, so that nothing would be changed in regard to Daniel."

Security

Ownership

Authority

Romans 8:38-39 — "I am convinced that neither death, nor life, nor angels, nor principalities, nor things present, nor things to come, nor powers, nor height, nor depth, nor any other created thing, will be able to separate us from the love of God, which is in Christ Jesus our Lord."

Security

Ownership

Authority

Revelation 5:1-3 — "I saw in the right hand of Him who sat on the throne a book written inside and on the back, sealed up with seven seals. And I saw a strong angel proclaiming with a loud voice, 'Who is worthy to open the book and to break its seals?' And no one in heaven or on the earth or under the earth was able to open the book or to look into it."

Security

Ownership

Authority

2. Read the following passage and identify its connection to your purpose and calling.

For this reason I too, having heard of the faith in the Lord Jesus which exists among you and your love for all the saints, do not cease giving thanks for you, while making mention of you in my prayers; that the God of our Lord Jesus Christ, the Father of glory, may give to you a spirit of wisdom and of revelation in the knowledge of Him. I pray that the eyes of your heart may be enlightened, so that you will know what is the hope of His calling, what are the riches of the glory of His inheritance in the saints, and what is the surpassing greatness of His power toward us who believe (Ephesians 1:15-19).

Why did Paul pray that the eyes of their hearts would be enlightened?

How do each of the three concepts of the "seal of the Spirit" give rise to someone living out their kingdom calling?

In chapter 9 of *The Power of the Holy Spirit's Names* book, Tony explains this more fully:

> The Holy Spirit will enable and empower you to know the hope of your calling. He will strengthen you to know the riches of the glory of the inheritance you're due as a follower of Jesus Christ.
>
> The Holy Spirit will also give you the ability to access the surpassing greatness of His power, and He does this by enlightening you. He informs your human spirit with His wisdom through the revelation and knowledge of Him. In doing so, you are released to experience more of God's reality in your life.
>
> *The Power of the Holy Spirit's Names,* page 148

What would you like to be "released to experience" in your life, regarding God's calling and purpose for you?

3. Read together Song of Solomon 8:6:

> Put me like a seal over your heart, like a seal on your arm. For love is as strong as

death, jealousy is as severe as Sheol; its flashes are flashes of fire, the very flame of the LORD.

What impressions do you get about the power of a "seal" from this verse?

Describe what it means to you to set a "seal over your heart."

What does a "seal on your arm" translate to in contemporary culture?

How do both of these seals (over your heart and on your arm) describe the Holy Spirit's role in our lives?

In Closing

As you end this session today, talk about this important but often overlooked subject of the "seal" of the Holy Spirit. Share any new insights or illustrations that came to you while going over this content.

Before session 6, complete the "On Your Own Between Sessions" section below.

On Your Own Between Sessions

1. God desires for you to live out the fullness of your kingdom calling and purpose. How do we know that? Because we are told in Ephesians 2:10:

   > We are His workmanship, created in Christ Jesus for good works, which God prepared beforehand so that we would walk in them.

   You have been chosen for good works God prepared for you ahead of time. List the three concepts concerning the Holy Spirit's sealing of you (we looked at them earlier in the group time).

   1. _____

   2. _____

   3. _____

   How do they play a part in your fulfilling your life purpose?

2. Life Exercise: Take Time in the Word of God

   One way to fully maximize the Holy Spirit's role in your life so you can maximize your own spiritual productivity is to spend time in His presence through reading the Bible, the Word of God.

   Intentionally set aside time each day over the course of the next week to read any part of the Bible you choose. You might read a whole chapter or even a whole book. It's totally up to you, but trust the process. God can work through His Word in your life, but you need to give Him the opportunity to do so by reading it.

   When you're done reading His Word, ask the Holy Spirit to bring to your mind what concepts from the Word relate to your personal calling. Ask Him to give you wisdom, then write down what you hear from the Spirit.

If time allows during next week's group meeting, share what you learned from the Spirit and how you sought to apply it in your life.

3. Reflect on the Scripture we explored as we started this week's session—Ephesians 1:13-14: "In Him, you also, after listening to the message of truth, the gospel of your salvation—having also believed, you were sealed in Him with the Holy Spirit of promise, who is given as a pledge of our inheritance, with a view to the redemption of God's own possession, to the praise of His glory."

Now ponder the various points of that passage:

- The seal is according to a promise.
- The Spirit is given as a "pledge of our inheritance."
- God owns us and has a view to redeem us.
- Our lives are to be lived in such a way that brings praise to His glory.

How do these principles show up in your daily life choices?

How can you more fully incorporate this perspective and mindset into your thoughts, words, and choices?

4. Reflection: Surrendering to the Sealing of the Spirit

How seriously do you take the three concepts the seal of the Spirit demonstrates—security, ownership, and authority?

Consider whether you can sharpen your thoughts on these three areas in order to gain a greater courage and power to live out your life purpose. Write down an action step you can take this week to move you one step closer to fulfilling your kingdom destiny.

Recommended Reading

In preparation for session 6, read chapters 10–12 of *The Power of the Holy Spirit's Names* book.

THE POWER

The following is an excerpt from *The Power of the Holy Spirit's Names* book, focusing on the Holy Spirit as the Power.

The attribute of power is one of the most misunderstood and under-utilized aspects of the Holy Spirit. The Holy Spirit is a powerful member of the Trinity. He takes from God the power that is God's and delivers it to you and me so that the power of heaven is made available to us in history.

While Jesus spoke of the kingdom and God's kingdom agenda, which is the visible manifestation of the comprehensive rule of God over every area of life, He also let the disciples know that the return of this kingdom would have to wait for some time. In the meantime, though, His followers were to be vested with the power to carry out God's kingdom agenda while on earth. And in essence, when Jesus did that, through the Holy Spirit, He supplied us with kingdom electricity to bring about God's overarching goal in history.

I once had a problem with the heating unit in my home. It wasn't working, it was in the dead of winter, and I was freezing. I called in a repair person and told him I thought I needed a new heating unit altogether. I assumed the whole thing was broken. But he took one look at my unit and said, "It's fine. Your ignitor just went out." It was a simple fix to a huge problem. All he needed to do was light a small piece of equipment inside the unit, which then lit the pilot so the flame could flow.

The Holy Spirit is our ignitor. He must be lit and allowed to burn fully within us in order for us to experience His power. No amount of church attendance, Bible study, attending small groups, or reading devotions will place you on the pathway of your kingdom purpose if the ignitor of the Holy Spirit has gone out. The Holy Spirit is responsible for empowering you to display the power within you.

Have you ever been left on the side of the road because your car battery went dead? That happened to me once. I'll never forget standing there with my car's hood up. After a while, someone kind stopped and offered to jump-start my car. He took the jumper cables from his own car and hooked them up to mine in order to transfer power. Even though I possessed the manual that explained what I needed to do when my car battery died, I couldn't revive it with information alone. My car wasn't about to move until someone transferred the power I needed.

The Bible contains all of the information we need in order to live our lives to the full. But if we're not properly hooked up to the Holy Spirit, it won't mean anything. We won't be able to go anywhere. Information without power is just information. The Holy Spirit must supply the power we need in order to enable us to use it. Without Him, we are spiritually stuck.

The Power of the Holy Spirit's Names, pages 170-172

Video Teaching Notes

As you watch the video, use the space below to take notes. Some key points and quotes are provided as reminders.

Main Idea

- Knowing facts and trying to be a good person will only get us so far. We need actual power to be able to live out our calling. As one of the members of the Trinity, the Holy Spirit offers the power of God to those whom He indwells, those who trust in Jesus, in order to equip us to carry out God's kingdom agenda.

- The Holy Spirit brings divine power to do God's work.

- The degree to which we stay connected to the Spirit is the degree to which we are able to effectively carry out our mission.

- The Holy Spirit's purpose is to glorify Jesus, not to glorify us. Let glorifying Jesus be our goal too.

- Personal Notes:

Application

Identify where you see the Spirit moving and working in your life and world, and then ask Him to empower you to obey and step out in an area you typically would fear.

Quotables

- When we accepted Jesus Christ, we were created to be children of God and to perform the work of God in order to advance the purposes of God.

- It is the job of the Holy Spirit to take the truth of God's Word and lift it into our experiences on a personal level…so we see it working and not merely as the information about what it's designed to do.

- Every believer is connected to the person and "power" of the Holy Spirit, but not every believer has the switch turned on because they are not kingdom oriented.

Video Group Discussion

1. Tony began this video session by talking about the various appliances we all have in our homes. He said, "They perform different duties as specified by the manufacturer, but one thing you can bank on: They're all drawing from the same power source." He goes on to say that if the power source is removed, the ability for the appliances to function will be gone as well. Identify a variety of spiritual gifts in the body of Christ.

   -
   -
   -
   -

   Describe how God's Spirit empowers each gift differently.

   Do you really want to do something but lack the personal courage or power to do it and could use the power of the Spirit to help you? Share what that is and how the Spirit could empower you.

Read Matthew 19:26:

> Looking at them Jesus said to them, "With people this is impossible, but with God all things are possible."

Share about a time when you felt something was impossible but God provided a way by opening a door for you, providing financial help you didn't expect, giving you endurance, or in some other way.

2. In the video, Tony said, "When Jesus was about to go back to heaven, He told His followers then, and His followers now that 'to pull off My purpose, you're going to need My power.'" He then goes on to talk about the passages in Scripture that illustrate this reality. How does Luke 24:49 below illustrate the need for the manifesting power of Christ through the presence of the Spirit before doing kingdom work?

> "Behold, I am sending forth the promise of My Father upon you; but you are to stay in the city until you are clothed with power from on high."

3. Tony also said in the video, "The Holy Spirit's job is to equip and enable believers to live out their kingdom calling—to experience the work and Word of God being lifted off of the pages of Scripture and being brought into their experience." In your own words, describe what it means to live out your "kingdom calling."

Can you think of a biblical example of someone who was empowered by the Spirit to live out his or her calling? What can you learn from this example?

How can a feeling of inadequacy or inability to do something related to your spiritual calling actually be a kingdom-prompt to pursue the power of the Spirit working through you?

When you experience these times of doubt concerning your own ability to live out your calling, what can you do to tap into the power of the Spirit?

4. Tony states an important principle in this video lesson:

> The role of the Holy Spirit is to give us as His children the ability, enablement, and empowerment to function as the followers of Christ that we have been created to be. And in order to pull this off, we've got to understand what goal this power is designed to accomplish. It's designed to take the truth of God and turn it into our experience.

What does it mean to "take the truth of God and turn it into our experience"? Can you identify a time when the truth of the Bible came alive to you on a personal and practical level? What did you learn from that experience?

To talk about how you're going to accomplish the God-sized dreams God has placed in your heart, do you first go to yourself or to your friends for support, or to the Spirit? What can you modify in your daily life to make going to the Spirit for power in living out your spiritual destiny the norm?

Group Bible Exploration

1. Chapter 11 in *The Power of the Holy Spirit's Names* says,

   The disciples wanted to know when Jesus would be returning to set up His kingdom. Jesus told them it was not for them to know. God was not revealing that
   information at that time. But what He did want them to know was that even
   though He was leaving them in His physical presence, He was still going to share
   His power with them. What Jesus left behind when He ascended into heaven was
   the person of the Holy Spirit, who would transfer spiritual power to each of us.

   The Power of the Holy Spirit's Names, page 170

   Read Acts 1:6-8:

   When they had come together, they were asking [Jesus], saying, "Lord, is it at this
   time You are restoring the kingdom to Israel?" He said to them, "It is not for you
   to know times or epochs which the Father has fixed by His own authority; but you
   will receive power when the Holy Spirit has come upon you; and you shall be My
   witnesses both in Jerusalem, and in all Judea and Samaria, and even to the remotest part of the earth."

   What does the "power" of the Spirit enable a person to do?

   What do you think Jesus meant by "be My witnesses"?

   How does the overall principle in Acts 1:6-8 connect with the Great Commission (Matthew 28:16-20)?

2. Read together Luke 11:13 and then 2 Corinthians 12:9:

> If you then, being evil, know how to give good gifts to your children, how much more will your heavenly Father give the Holy Spirit to those who ask Him?

> He has said to me, "My grace is sufficient for you, for power is perfected in weakness." Most gladly, therefore, I will rather boast about my weaknesses, so that the power of Christ may dwell in me.

Oftentimes we're called to do the work of God where we feel the least able to do it on our own. With his church, Tony has shared that as a child he couldn't form a complete sentence because his stuttering was so bad. But God somehow called him to be a professional speaker as a pastor. Why do you think God will often lead us into a kingdom calling where we don't feel personally skilled or empowered on our own?

Based on the Scripture passages above, what do we need to do to access the power of the Spirit in order to live out the will of God?

3. Read together Acts 2:1-4:

> When the day of Pentecost had come, they were all together in one place. And suddenly there came from heaven a noise like a violent rushing wind, and it filled the whole house where they were sitting. And there appeared to them tongues as of fire distributing themselves, and they rested on each one of them. And they were all filled with the Holy Spirit and began to speak with other tongues, as the Spirit was giving them utterance.

What is the transforming effect of the Spirit in this passage?

What did the disciples go on to do after receiving the power of the Spirit?

In what ways are you relying on the Spirit's power to live out your kingdom calling?

How do you feel when you experience the Holy Spirit empowering you to do what you never thought you could do?

4. Read together Hebrews 10:23-25:

> Let us hold fast the confession of our hope without wavering, for He who promised is faithful; and let us consider how to stimulate one another to love and good deeds, not forsaking our own assembling together, as is the habit of some, but encouraging one another; and all the more as you see the day drawing near.

In practical, contemporary examples, what does it mean to not forsake "our own assembling together"?

What are some positive outcomes when people gather to talk about the Bible, the Spirit's work in their lives, and the "good deeds" they're seeking to live out?

Why do you think the writer of Hebrews emphasized our gathering together so we can be about "encouraging one another"?

In Closing

As you end this study, remember these things:

1. Access the power of the Spirit through a heart of honesty, gratitude, and awareness of His presence.

2. Commit to lean on the Spirit's power rather than on your own—even ask Him how to do that better than you do now.

3. Seek to gather with like-minded believers to talk about God's Word and what the Spirit is doing in and through your lives.

4. Bust free from your comfort zone and use the power of the Spirit available to you.

5. Honor God's calling in your life by walking in step with the Holy Spirit day by day.

You have everything you need to fully experience the abundant Christian life Jesus has given to you (John 10:10). God won't force it on you, but it's available to you through your relationship with the Holy Spirit. As you close out this study, encourage one another to remain committed to the pursuit of an ever-growing and deepening experience of the Spirit.

Close in prayer, mindful to thank God for all He has done in and through your life and the lives of those with whom you've gathered for this study. Ask Him to give you wisdom about what to study and apply next.

THE URBAN ALTERNATIVE

The Urban Alternative (TUA) equips, empowers, and unites Christians to impact individuals, families, churches, and communities through a thoroughly kingdom-agenda worldview. In teaching truth, we seek to transform lives.

The core cause of the problems we face in our personal lives, homes, churches, and societies is a spiritual one. Therefore, the only way to address that core cause is spiritually. We've tried a political, social, economic, and even a religious agenda, and now it's time for a kingdom agenda.

The kingdom agenda can be defined as the visible manifestation
of the comprehensive rule of God over every area of life.

The unifying central theme throughout the Bible is the glory of God and the advancement of His kingdom. The conjoining thread from Genesis to Revelation—from beginning to end—is focused on one thing: God's glory through advancing God's kingdom.

When we do not recognize that theme, the Bible becomes for us a series of disconnected stories that are great for inspiration but seem to be unrelated in purpose and direction. Understanding the role of the kingdom in Scripture increases our understanding of the relevancy of this several-thousand-year-old text to our day-to-day living. That's because God's kingdom was not only then; it is now.

The absence of the kingdom's influence in our personal lives, family lives, churches, and communities has led to a deterioration in our world of immense proportions:

- People live segmented, compartmentalized lives because they lack God's kingdom worldview.

- Families disintegrate because they exist for their own satisfaction rather than for the kingdom.

- Churches are limited in the scope of their impact because they fail to comprehend that the goal of the church is not the church itself but the kingdom.

- Communities have nowhere to turn to find real solutions for real people who have real problems because the church has become divided, in-grown, and unable to transform the cultural and political landscape in any relevant way.

By optimizing the solutions of heaven, the kingdom agenda offers us a way to see and live life with a solid hope. When God is no longer the final and authoritative standard under which all else falls, order and hope have left with Him. But the reverse of that is true as well: as long as we have God, we have hope. If God is still in the picture, and as long as His agenda is still on the table, it's not over.

Even if relationships collapse, God will sustain us. Even if finances dwindle, God will keep us. Even if dreams die, God will revive us. As long as God and His rule are still the overarching standard in our lives, families, churches, and communities, there is always hope.

Our world needs the King's agenda. Our churches need the King's agenda. Our families need the King's agenda.

We've put together a three-part plan to direct us to heal the divisions and strive for unity as we move toward the goal of truly being one nation under God. This three-part plan calls us to assemble with others in unity, to address the issues that divide us, and to act together for social impact. Following this plan, we will see individuals, families, churches, and communities transformed as we follow God's kingdom agenda in every area of our lives. You can request this plan by emailing Info@TonyEvans.org or by going online to TonyEvans.org.

In many major cities, drivers can take a loop to the other side of the city when they don't want to head straight through downtown. This loop takes them close enough to the city center so they can see its towering buildings and skyline but not close enough to actually experience it.

This is precisely what we, as a culture, have done with God. We have put Him on the "loop" of our personal, family, church, and community lives. He's close enough to be at hand should we need Him in an emergency but far enough away that He can't be the center of who we are. We want God on the "loop," not the King of the Bible who comes downtown into the very heart of our ways. And as we have seen in our own lives and in the lives of others, leaving God on the "loop" brings about dire consequences.

But when we make God, and His rule, the centerpiece of all we think, do, or say, we experience Him in the way He longs for us to experience Him. He wants us to be kingdom people with kingdom minds set on fulfilling His kingdom's purposes. He wants us to pray, as Jesus did, "Not My will, but Thy will be done" because His is the kingdom, the power, and the glory.

There is only one God, and we are not Him. As King and Creator, God calls the shots. Only when we align ourselves under His comprehensive hand will we access His full power and authority in all spheres of life: personal, familial, ecclesiastical, and governmental.

As we learn how to govern ourselves under God, we then transform the institutions of family, church, and society using a biblically based kingdom worldview.

Under Him, we touch heaven and change earth.

To achieve our goal, we use a variety of strategies, approaches, and resources for reaching and equipping as many people as possible.

Broadcast Media

Millions of individuals experience *The Alternative with Dr. Tony Evans*, a daily broadcast on nearly 1,400 radio outlets and in more than 130 countries. The broadcast can also be seen on several television networks and is available online at TonyEvans.org. As well, you can listen to or view the daily broadcast by downloading the Tony Evans app for free in the App Store. Over 30,000,000 message downloads/streams occur each year.

Leadership Training

The Tony Evans Training Center (TETC) facilitates a comprehensive discipleship platform, which provides an educational program that embodies the ministry philosophy of Dr. Tony Evans as expressed through the kingdom agenda. The training courses focus on leadership development and discipleship in the following five tracks:

1. Bible & Theology
2. Personal Growth
3. Family and Relationships
4. Church Health and Leadership Development
5. Society and Community Impact Strategies

The TETC program includes courses for both local and online students. Furthermore, TETC programming includes course work for non-student attendees. Pastors, Christian leaders, and Christian laity—both local and at a distance—can seek out the Kingdom Agenda Certificate for personal, spiritual, and professional development. For more information, visit TonyEvansTraining.org

Kingdom Agenda Pastors (KAP) provides a viable network for like-minded pastors who embrace the kingdom agenda philosophy. Pastors have the opportunity to go deeper with Dr. Tony Evans as they are given greater biblical knowledge, practical applications, and resources to impact individuals, families, churches, and communities. KAP welcomes senior and associate pastors of all churches. KAP also offers an annual Summit held each year in Dallas with intensive seminars, workshops, and resources. For more information, visit KAFellowship.org.

Pastors' Wives Ministry, founded by the late Dr. Lois Evans, provides counsel, encouragement, and spiritual resources for pastors' wives as they serve with their husbands in the ministry. A primary focus of the ministry is the KAP Summit, where senior pastors' wives have a safe place to reflect, renew, and relax along with receiving training in personal development, spiritual growth, and care for their emotional and physical well-being. For more information, visit LoisEvans.org.

Kingdom Community Impact

The outreach programs of The Urban Alternative seek to provide positive impact on individuals, churches, families, and communities through a variety of ministries. We see these efforts as necessary to our calling as a ministry and essential to the communities we serve. With training on how to initiate and maintain programs to adopt schools, provide homeless services, and partner toward unity and justice with the local police precincts, which creates a connection between the police and our community, we, as a ministry, live out God's kingdom agenda according to our *Kingdom Strategy for Community Transformation*.

The *Kingdom Strategy for Community Transformation* is a three-part plan that equips churches to have a positive impact on their communities for the kingdom of God. It also provides numerous practical suggestions for how this three-part plan can be implemented in your community, and it serves as a blueprint for unifying churches around the common goal of creating a better world for all of us. For more information, visit TonyEvans.org, then click on the link to access the 3-Point Plan. A course for this strategy is also offered online through the Tony Evans Training Center.

Tony Evans Films ushers in positive life change through compelling video-shorts, animation, and feature-length films. We seek to build kingdom disciples through the power of story. We use a variety of platforms for viewer consumption and have 120,000,000+ digital views. We also merge video-shorts and film with relevant Bible study materials to bring people to the saving knowledge of Jesus Christ and to strengthen the body of Christ worldwide. Tony Evans Films released its first feature-length film, *Kingdom Men Rising*, in April 2019 in more than 800 theaters nationwide in partnership with Lifeway Films. The second release, *Journey with Jesus*, is in partnership with RightNow Media and was released in theaters in November 2021.

Resource Development

By providing a variety of published materials, we are fostering lifelong learning partnerships with the people we serve. Dr. Evans has published more than 125 unique titles based on more than 50 years of preaching—in booklet, book, or Bible study format. He also holds the honor of writing and publishing the first full-Bible commentary and study Bible by an African American, released in 2019. This Bible sits in permanent display as a historic release in the Museum of the Bible in Washington, DC.

For more information and a complimentary copy of Dr. Evans's devotional newsletter, call (800) 800-3222 or write to TUA at P.O. Box 4000, Dallas TX 75208, or visit us online at:

www.TonyEvans.org

To learn more about Harvest House books and
to read sample chapters, visit our website:

www.HarvestHousePublishers.com

HARVEST HOUSE PUBLISHERS
EUGENE, OREGON